All glory to God. Not me, but Christ in me. Any good I do is not of my own hands but His grace, mercy, love, and guidance. *(Galatians 2:20)*

Acclaim For Julia Rose

He Is Faithful In Every Season

"In reading the carefully and artfully crafted words of Julia Rose, I couldn't help but enter moments of prayer and reflection. I appreciate that these poems come across as music to the heart given their lyrical quality and devotion to God." *-Christian Shelves*

"I felt and related to Julia's poems that convey fear, doubt, hope, and the belief in redemption, and I am decades her senior." *-Goodreads Review*

"All poems point clearly to Jesus as being the center of everything, using beautiful language to heighten the understanding of the Gospel." *-Rob Seabrook, Author of Beneath the Tamarisk Tree*

"Whether you've been a believer in Christ for many years, or are just starting your faith journey, this collection of poems has images and literary devices that make each poem easy to relate to and connect with." *-Goodreads Review*

"These [poems] are absolutely Psalm-like in nature and highly relatable, infused with passion and depth, challenging readers to take their trials and turn them into fuel for a pursuit of Jesus." *-Ashley W., Literary Agent*

Who I Was

"God sent me Julia Rose in a package ministering to my spirit during my difficult valley. The cadence and rhythm are just so powerful. I feel like scales have fallen off my eyes." *-Lara Silverman, Author of Singing Through Fire*

"*Who I Was* questions the reader's walk in life, uplifts, motivates, and is relatable, while also emphasizing Jesus Christ and the Father." *-Beta Reader*

"If you find yourself struggling with sin, discouraged by feeling like a disappointment, or disliking yourself after receiving God's grace, this book is both a mirror and a beacon of hope by showing that you're not alone while pointing to the One who completely shapes and molds us as a result of who we have been." *-Christian Shelves*

"The way Julia explores the concept [self-love] is humble and transparent, truly a journey the readers can join with her in growth! She shares so much wisdom and reflection on a topic that is so debated and misunderstood today." *-Beta Reader*

"I resonated deeply with many of the poems and couldn't help but praise God through the entire reading. Julia's devotionals are equally powerful and encouraging, feeding my soul and furthering my understanding of the Lord's goodness." *-Goodreads Review*

Other Books by Julia Rose

Poetry

He Is Faithful In Every Season

Who I Was

A Collection of Poetry and Devotionals

By Julia Rose

Who I Was

Cover design by Julia Rose with Canva Pro.

Formatting and editing by Julia Rose, www.juliarosebooks.com

ISBN: 979-8-218-84500-1 (paperback)
ISBN: 979-8-218-84501-8 (ebook)

Published by Julia Rose Books

First Edition 2025

To the God Who showed me where my worth and beauty come from—*Jesus*.

"And God saw everything that He had made, and behold, it was very good." Genesis 1:31a

Before Jesus, I Was:

Anxious, ignorant, judgmental,

lukewarm, empty, self-centered,

untrusting, lethargic, hopeless,

aimless, searching, self-hating,

lost, doubtful, easily misled,

lustful, always turning a blind eye,

a sinner.

With Jesus, I Am:

Set free.

Saved by grace.

No longer lost.

Identified by love.

Changed.

Table of Contents

Foreword

It is a huge honor to be writing this foreword. However, I will admit to feeling woefully under-qualified in light of what you will read in this book.

When Julia first asked me to write this, I was shocked. Mostly because I couldn't imagine writing anything that would add to what she has already written. But here I go.

I suppose I should start by explaining my relationship with Julia. I met her a little over two years ago, when we worked together at a Christian bookstore. It didn't take long to see we would be more than coworkers. Over the next few years, we became great friends. (Honestly, I'm not convinced there's anyone who wouldn't want to be Julia's friend.) The love of Jesus pours from Julia, not just in her writing, but in her actions every day. I can say with certainty, there is nothing she puts to paper that she does not also strive to live.

Her poetry is a shining beacon in a sea of secular writing, infused with a rawness and theological depth that is amazing. She doesn't shy away from human condition, nor does she withhold the truth of the gospel. I could go on and on about how wonderful Julia is, but I'm going to refrain. Because ultimately, to God be the glory. This book will attest to the fact that every believer truly has no good they can lay claim to on their own. We are all the partakers of a grace so much bigger than ourselves.

Reading *Who I Was* has been deeply encouraging to me. It is a beautiful testimony to a believer's transformation from sinner to saint. My prayer is that this book uplifts every believer who reads it, exhorting us to reflect on the great gift we have been given. In a world that is so self-absorbed, the children of God are given the unique privilege of looking to Someone beyond themselves.

Jesus is our identity, believer.

Let the reality of that truth sink in—with all its implications.

Everything Jesus is, we can lay claim to in Him. The Father not only doesn't see our sin, but sees Jesus in place of us. That is an astounding truth. God doesn't pretend we are righteous—He declares it. We often think of the cross as our "not guilty" verdict. But it is so much more. It is a banner that hangs over our lives, declaring we have always stayed in step with the law of God.

Friend, this reality should humble us beyond measure. If anyone can look at that gift and be proud of themselves, I would venture to say they have not yet grasped the extraordinary reality that is the cross of Christ. For truly, as sinners, we bring nothing to Jesus except the insurmountable debt we owe. I pray this book is not just a read, but a journey. Let it be an opportunity to remember and a call to praise for who we are now compared to who we once were. And let it push us to tell others. This grace is a free invitation, and there is a hurting world out there in desperate need of this message.

We are living in an identity war, and our society is losing the fight. Our culture tells us to look inward for what can only be found outside of ourselves. Jesus is good news. More than that, He is the best news for our world. People are constantly being told that, to escape the weight of our sin, we must esteem ourselves more. But that is hardly the case. Alternatively, it is equally wrong to employ self-destructive means to assuage our conscience.

We find our identity by being hidden in Christ. Only then can we flourish. Only then can the human soul begin to breathe new life.

Who I Was faithfully reminds us to live in the confidence of our new identity, leaving behind the old life we've been redeemed from. Jesus paid much too high a price for us to live the way we were. Julia invites us on a journey with her —not of self-discovery, but of God-discovery. For only in Him do we find who we truly are. He knows us best, and my prayer is that we can learn to see ourselves through the eyes of our loving Father.

This is our story.

This is our testimony.

As believers, we can say with confidence, this was *Who I Was*, but God…

"But God, being rich in mercy, because of the great love with which He loved us, even when we were dead in our trespasses, made us alive together with Christ—by grace you have been saved—and raised us up with Him and seated us with Him in the heavenly places in Christ Jesus, so that in the coming ages He might show the immeasurable riches of His grace in kindness toward us in Christ Jesus. For by grace you have been saved through faith. And this is not your own doing; it is the gift of God, not a result of works, so that no one may boast." Ephesians 2:4-8

Soli Deo Gloria.

-Addison Jean, Friend, Artist, Writer, CVA, Animal-lover

Author's Note

When I was first convicted of my sin, I hated myself. I hated how blind and lukewarm I was. I hated how quickly I'd fall into satan's traps. I've always struggled with seeing myself through God's eyes, whether it be thinking too highly of myself and slipping into vanity, or loathing myself and discarding my identity in Christ. But when my eyes were opened to my sin, instead of accepting God's forgiveness, I'd dwell on what He saved me from.

I fell into this self-hatred pattern that was a chore to rid. To me, loving myself was a product of the world. Society's idea of "self-love" was sinful, for are we not called to be humble? *(James 4:10)*. Yet, God has been teaching me that sin has twisted our relationship with "self" as it has our relationship with God. But when Jesus died on the cross and rose again, restoring the relationship between us and God, all others followed—relationships with people, creation, and, yes, even ourselves. Unfortunately, sin has warped the concept of self-love, polluting a notion God designed long ago. Jesus Himself said to *"love your neighbor as yourself." (Matt. 22:39)*. While the world says, "Love *only* yourself, and put yourself first, above all."

I find there are two spectrums of the "self-love" idea. One is where love is nonexistent, and the person hates themselves to the point of neglect. While on the other hand, all a person can see is themselves, and in turn, they ignore others, which inevitably leads to them neglecting themselves. Both are rooted in pride. Self-hatred stems from the mindset that no one cares or we're not good enough. It may not seem prideful, but even when utterly loathing ourselves, are we not thinking *only* of ourselves? As for those who gladly love themselves without a thought for others, pride is at the center of that life, too. It all comes back to where our focus is.

Us, or *Jesus?*

Does it all end in self-sabotage, and can we truly find the balance between vanity and disdain for oneself?

When did "self-love" become so misconstrued?

Where can we go to find the truth about a concept so idolized by the world?

How do we love ourselves in a way that would honor God? Is it by gawking in the mirror and primping our appearance? Is it by hiding in isolation to avoid making a mistake? Or is "self-love" something more? Perhaps it's acknowledging that anything we have to love about ourselves isn't *ourselves* but who God designed us to be.

His image bearers.

I'm writing this note while I struggle with my own "self-love" issues, though I use this term loosely and a bit warily, knowing how the world has destroyed the prospect. I'm not referring to selfish, egotistical love. I'm talking about a love that acknowledges the beauty of a creature crafted by its Creator. A selfless, humble love. The kind of love that's emphasized in *Matthew 22:37-38*. Before Jesus tells us to *"love your neighbor as yourself,"* He says, *"You shall love the Lord your God with all your heart and with all your soul and with all your mind. This is the great and first commandment."*

To love others and ourselves well, we need to love God *first*. He needs to be at the center of everything, even this.

The hardest part about hating myself is the fact that I know where my identity is found. I proudly bear the name of Christ and believe who He's called me to be. But oftentimes, I find myself frustrated by my faults and mistakes, infuriated by what I'm incapable of doing, and constantly comparing myself to others. Those flaws are all I can see, and I'm tempted to return to old habits of self-hatred. Only by God's strength and wisdom am I learning to love myself in a way that would please and glorify Him, so that I can better love others, but most importantly, love Him above all else.

That's why I wrote *Who I Was*. Because God suddenly opened my eyes to the lack of truth regarding our identity and where we attach ourselves.

Is it even possible? Can we truly love ourselves in a way that isn't vain, conceited, or narcissistic?

I believe so, and I'm learning how. But, as a disclosure, this book is not one with all the answers. Instead, it points to the One Who knows all. It portrays my personal testimony to being completely changed by Jesus and explores the truth of who we are in Christ and what it means to love Him more than anything. And, though it wasn't my intention, this book is catered more towards women simply because it's written from the perspective of one, though men are welcome to journey through this book as well. I just urge you to understand one thing:

This isn't some self-help, self-love, focus-on-you type of book. No, this is about *Who* our identity is linked to.

Spoiler, it's the Creator of the Universe.

I find it incredible and humorous that God has planted another poetry book in my heart, this one pinpointing our identity in Christ and the beauty of being transformed from the inside out by the Holy Spirit. I didn't plan to draft a book on this widely misinterpreted movement, not with my track record of hating and idolizing myself.

I admit, I feel disqualified to write a book on such truth, one I'm still learning and struggling to hold on to, especially as I continue battling insecurity, self-loathing, and ignorance. But, maybe, that's the point. Perhaps my lack of qualification is just the thing to further illuminate the power and faithfulness of God. Either way, I can't ignore how God led me to write this book. Apart from my personal struggles, I've witnessed my friends fall from their identity in Christ and struggle to see themselves through His eyes. I've heard the self-loathing come from their lips, or from the conversations I've had with my sisters, mom, and other women in my life. In church, over and over, it seemed God was gently reminding me of my identity in Him through sermons and classes that discussed the beauty of God's design and His astounding love to create. My heart ached to see the overwhelming attacks on our identities, and then followed a curious thought I couldn't shake:

If I fail to love myself as God does, how can I ever love others the same way?

I hope you find through this book that the love we have for ourselves shouldn't come from *us* but from the loving God Who intimately designed us. If you look in the mirror and hate what you see, or look too long in vanity; if you pick apart every word you said, or care too much about sharing your opinion; if you ask God, "Why did you make me this way?" or believe yourself to be perfect; if you despise your personality and quirks, or place yourself on a pedestal; if you question your identity, or find it in your performance and appearance, this book is for you.

The idolaters and haters of "self."

We all fall into one of the two. Maybe a mix of both. But like anything, there is a balance between "saved by grace" and "wretched sinner." Yes, we are redeemed, loved, set free, and covered by the blood of Jesus. However, we soon find in Scripture that we aren't "free to do as we please." We are far from perfect, simply freed from being enslaved to what we were once blinded to—*our sin*.

I pray the following poems and devotionals redirect you to the One Who has called you by name. You are irrevocably, undeniably, and truly loved by the God Who created the heavens and the earth—*your* Designer. He knows us better than anyone. Should we not then go to *Him* for advice on how to love ourselves to better love others?

Join me as we learn, *together*, what it means to see ourselves through the loving eyes of Jesus. Before we begin this journey, let me pray for us:

"God, we surrender and ask for Your help. Whether we are struggling to love ourselves or love only ourselves, guide us in the direction that will best honor You. Open our eyes,

Jesus, to the things we cannot see. The things keeping us from enjoying the beauty You want us to partake in here on earth until eternity. Lord, I ask You to use Your Holy Spirit to fill our hearts with an undeniable gratitude for all You've accomplished on the cross so that we can be here today in a relationship with You. I pray over these poems and words, that they may be used for Your kingdom to equip and inspire those who have forgotten where their identity lies— *in You.* Thank You for creating us in Your image and for allowing us to live a life in the shelter of Your presence and mercy. It's in Your name I pray, Jesus. Amen."

Potter

Nothing
that's all there was,
empty darkness
until the Potter spoke life.

Dust
no form or shape,
limp and purposeless
until it met the Potter's plan.

Clay
needing to be crafted,
lacking life and joy
until it met the Potter's hand.

Life
formed and molded,
filled with light and hope,
no longer lacking.

To dust, we all return,
for are we not made

for Him and by Him?
Let us then live to worship.

Does the statue say
to its sculptor,
"Why did you carve me
this way?"

Does the canvas say
to its painter,
"Why am I like this?
I hate my color."

Does the vase say
to its shaper,
"Why must I hold flowers?
Can't I be something else?"

As a creature of the God
of the universe,
why do we question all
we were made to do?

Sculpted by the Potter,

shaped and formed in the void;
seen without any form yet loved,
known before entering the world.

God, if we question You in spite,
may we be struck humble,
for at Your feet and in Your
hands are where we were made.

Who are we to question our purpose
as if we know best in terms of
what we're made for?
Who are we to question the Creator?

A weapon does not balk at being used
nor a book glare for being read;
a shovel does not wish to be a bowl
nor a bird beg to be a crustacean.

Are not all things designed by You,
all for their own God-given purpose?
May we be reminded of our place,
how we came from nothing but ashes.

Devotional

"But now, O LORD, You are our Father; we are the clay, and You are the potter; we are all the work of Your hand." Isaiah 64:8

Key Takeaway: We are made for God

Each person has a longing to know their purpose. But it's simpler than what we make it out to be. Our purpose is *Him*. We were formed to be in a relationship with Him, made to worship and love Him. God doesn't need us, yet He chooses to use us. He created us knowing we'd fail, gave us free will to voluntarily love Him in return. Our hearts find satisfaction and fulfillment when doing what they were made to do. We were made from dust, after all, and to dust we will return *(Genesis 3:19)*. However, despite knowing we are made for Him, we still question Him. We look straight at Him and have the audacity to ask why He'd make us a certain way or put us in a particular situation, as if our hearts didn't rely on His power to keep beating. Sometimes we get too caught up in what we're not doing and miss what God has been doing—drawing us closer to Him. God uses every stage of life to glorify His name in the highest. When we look at our lives in light of our purpose being to live for Him, everything we do from then on holds an eternal meaning. Nothing is meaningless in the hands of God.

"I'm Sorry"

The night was quiet.
I sat on my bed,
hands in my hair,
my heartbeat violent.

No sound but
the steady rhythm of
my fear and terror,
a chilling caress.

I didn't know what
was to be said or
what to pray;
I could just stare.

Another panic attack
another fear
another nightmare
another tear.

The words wouldn't come
at first, only silent tears,

hot against my skin;
my cries about to burst.

satan's evil cheers,
triumphing over my fear;
another painful win
after all these years.

But no, that's simply
another lie of his,
and oh, how quick I am
to believe it.

I whispered, "I'm sorry,"
over and over,
words too weak and empty
to ever cover my sin.

I hugged my trembling body
and rumpled my covers;
squirming in my own skin.
Only God can win.

I couldn't explain what I felt,

I only knew You knew,

and that alone gave me peace;

to have You cherish and see me.

The fear and shame melted

and Your faithfulness once again

stood true in the darkness;

I'm sorry mine is constantly discarded.

I hate it.

My sin

my failures

the evil temptations

and desires.

I. Hate. Them.

I hate letting satan get the

best of everything,

that which should be reserved

for God and eternity.

I hate believing his lies.

Why, oh why, do we do that?

In a world so twisted,

we must fight to never give in.

But if we were strong enough,

we'd never see our need for a Savior;

we'd be greedy and blind,

intoxicated by our features.

During times of weakness,

it's proof of our need for Jesus.

Evil is like a disease, something to

be disposed of before it consumes us.

Only the Lord can release us.

I hate how I forget that,

but I'm overjoyed God,

my Savior, is merciful;

He is forgiving and amazing.

How many days will we waste

trying to be perfect?

Trying to save ourselves

when Jesus has been given to us?

Our saving grace is not
through things we can do,
but rather, through the One
Who can do all.

I'm sorry, God,
for trying to leave,
for pushing *my* will
instead of submitting.

I'm sorry, God,
for all the times I've
attempted to be more
when it's You I adore.

And I'm sorry, God,
when I become conceited;
arrogant in my faith or
misguided and deceived.

I'm sorry for forgetting
my identity.

Devotional

"For by grace you have been saved through faith. And this is not your own doing; it is the gift of God, not a result of works, so that no one may boast."

Ephesians 2:8-9

Key Takeaway: God's grace is enough

One of the hardest parts about following Jesus is how we're still capable of sinning. After repenting, we may be free from the repercussions and guilt, but we can't disregard the fact that we still become trapped in the same old cycles. It's easy to begin to hate our evil deeds and mistakes, going as far as hating ourselves and the sins we struggled with and still do. But this is where the grace of God comes in. Different from mercy—which is refraining from giving us what we deserve—grace is a gift, something we could never earn. When blinded by our constant backsliding, we can forget this grace. We must tread carefully and not forget that, though our sin needs to be despised, it cannot be our primary focus. Jesus shed His blood, stepped into suffering, and became unrecognizable so that we would no longer have to gaze at our sins. Instead, they are opportunities for God to be glorified and for His grace to break through. We come to His feet, repent, and turn away. We turn to *Him* and rest in His grace, for it is enough *(2 Corinthians 12:9).*

Two Summers Ago

Two summers ago, when I had
fallen so low, all I could do was cry
as the days dragged on with
fear controlling my life.

Oh, two summers ago,
how I remember those days.
When I lost all control,
when anxiety took my life.

Choking me out from the inside,
filling my heart, soul, and mind;
poisoning my life with lies,
leaving me an empty shell.

All I could do was convulse in bed,
tense and afraid, trembling,
begging the panic to cease;
praying for the days to end.

Two summers ago,
when my smiles were pretend;

when I fought for joy and
when a war raged in my head.

It didn't matter where I looked,
didn't matter where I fell
because two summers ago,
I was lost and I was alone.

Darkness took over my mind.
I prayed and hoped I'd be fine,
but as the fear crept inside
I fell deeper into a horrifying life.

I was no longer living, but
watching from the sidelines;
everyone else was living
while I pretended to be fine.

No one noticed,
no one saw that I wasn't fine.
I struggled even to eat at all,
I fell apart behind my bedroom walls.

Two summers ago

I never thought I'd grow;
I had given up hope
thinking fear was my life now.

Panic attacks time after time,
nightmares, unable to escape the night;
chills and numbness entering my spine,
too exhausted to smile, too afraid to shine.

Two summers ago,
when I had lost all hope,
You were my light;
You rescued me from the fight.

You were always, never failing
to lift me when I crumbled.
You always cared and saw when
I was shaking, and when I trembled.

Two summers ago,
God, You saved my life;
pulled me out of darkness and
You rescued me from my mind.

Two summers ago,
when I thought I was alone,
You were walking beside me,
encouraging me to fight.

And now, *I will.*

I will fight with every breath,
piercing lies with truth;
I refuse to back down now,
for I am safe with You.

This summer I will
live life through the tears;
I will hold on to the fire,
this hope You've given me.

This summer I will
no longer let fear destroy
the freedom You died for
to gift me this peace and victory.

This summer I will work hard
and give You all praise and glory,

for the love You've blessed me with
has redeemed my broken story.

Because of You, I've grown this year
even with countless tears;
for two summers ago
Your love gave me hope.

You are making me strong and bold.

God, You made a way;
You broke through my chains,
You saved this beautiful life
and for You alone I choose to shine.

Not looking back at
two summers ago,
but looking forward to
this peace that won't let go.

I'm no longer that girl;
I am free and alive.
Thank You, Lord, for I would
never replace two summers ago.

For it's then, You changed my life.

Devotional

"Remember not the former things, nor consider the things of old. Behold, I am doing a new thing; now it springs forth, do you not perceive it? I will make a way in the wilderness and rivers in the desert." Isaiah 43:18-19

Key Takeaway: Our pasts don't define us

Shame, guilt, and disdain are common aftereffects of a changed life. We regret how we once lived, perhaps wishing time wasn't wasted on such triviality. If only we had given our lives to God sooner. But the thing is, God is the only One Who can open our eyes *(Luke 24:45)*. Yes, people are disobedient and choose not to follow Him. However, we can have hope knowing that those God chose cannot be kept from Him *(Romans 8:38-39)*. He opens our eyes on His own timing. God knew when and how we'd come to know Him, loving us at our darkest, making a way through the desert, and bridging the chasm that separates us from a relationship with Him. He knew our pasts before we were born and still sent His Son Jesus to bear the burden of our sins. He set us free from the past. Because of Jesus, we have a new identity. Our pasts shouldn't be seen in the light of shame but in *gratitude* for what God has saved us from. The stories of who we once were are testimonies of God's faithfulness, grace, and mercy.

Who Was I?

Who was I
before I met You?
How did I live
before I knew You?

What was life
when I was trapped
in the whims of culture
and anxious strife?

How did I live
walking so blind?
How did I breathe
with fear inside?

How did my life
reflect You, God?
What was my life
when I was living a lie?

By Your grace,
You've opened my eyes;

my life has changed
forever testifying to Your light.

Devotional

"So, because you are lukewarm, and neither hot nor cold, I will spit you out of my mouth." Revelation 3:16

Key Takeaway: Our faith needs to be worked out

The life of a lukewarm believer may be more tragic than that of a non-believer. Whereas an unbeliever has the opportunity to hear about Jesus, the lukewarm believer already has and does nothing but float on the surface of faith. It's an odd "in-between" state—not really knowing Jesus, but also wouldn't dream of committing particularly immoral sins. There's no depth in their faith, no relationship. Like the parable of the seeds and the sower *(Mark 4:2-9)*, when a seed of faith falls on good soil, it grows, and when it lands in thorns, it's choked up. This parable speaks to the fact that not everyone will be saved, but another way to look at it is: where are we throwing our seeds? Where are we putting our faith? Is it in something that will last, or in the temporary? If we don't constantly pursue God, we fail to grow in our relationship with Him. Every day is an opportunity to work out our faith *(James 2:17)* and avoid stagnant beliefs that are nothing more than empty words. Our walk with God was never meant to be one layer, but an infinite journey of depth.

Death Penalty

I am a criminal.

For many years, I've walked
a path of darkness and peril,
drawing myself in pride;
lusting after the extravagant.

My crimes are accounted for,
they cannot be ignored;
I know what my penalty will be,
for it's all that I deserve.

I walk to the podium
where the Judge towers above.
In chains and an orange jumpsuit,
I await what is to come.

Before me is displayed
all I've committed in the dark,
and even in the light, times I
thought no one else saw.

My life, every day, every hour,
rewound and played for all;
revealing my deepest regrets,
brandishing my rebellious soul.

The Judge orders me to sit,
and soon I'm chained to a table;
watching all my mistakes play out,
wondering how I could've done better.

The Judge sits high, gavel in hand;
justice burns His eyes and face,
for the wrath that I deserve
cannot be contained.

My sentence will be read
and I will get my penance;
all I've brought upon me and
the harm I've caused my loved ones.

My crimes are filthy,
deserving of the death penalty,
for I am the worst of sinners;
I don't deserve mercy.

I am guilty of sin,

ashamed of my desires;

I am chained to the dark,

lost and without power.

The Judge meets my eyes,

a storm of fury and sorrow;

I'm surprised to find tears

trailing down His cheeks.

It's then, I know my penalty.

For what else could it be

but death itself?

I have committed crimes

deserving of hell.

The gavel drops quickly,

racing towards the table,

as the Judge expels the verdict

I will soon have placed upon me.

But then, the jury begins to stir.

Movement breaks from

the crowd as it parts like a sea,
one lone Man singled out.

Just as the gavel falls,
seconds from hitting the wood,
the Man reaches His hand out,
snapping the mallet in two.

The wood splinters and falls,
landing hard on the ground
at the feet of the Judge, Who
gladly steps down from His throne.

I've never met this Man.
I don't recognize His face;
He's but a stranger, and yet,
I hear Him call my name.

I've never met this Man,
the One Who paused my penalty;
He walks toward me now,
His face an array of glory.

A smile stretches His lips,

the complete picture of peace;
as if He knew this day was coming,
as if He knew where I'd one day be.

He lifts a hand, and my shackles,
they tremble and unlock;
falling at my feet with a
bone-rattling, soul-stirring, shatter.

Then the Man gathers my chains
and places them around His own wrists,
binding Himself with my guilt;
taking on all I deserve.

He turns to face the Judge,
an innocent Man accepting
everything not belonging to Him;
absorbing blame that is not His.

Never once sinning, no,
a perfect life lived, yet,
simply to die for my own selfish
deeds and incompetence.

The Judge indicts the death penalty,
bestowing it upon this Man instead;
a path my life would've taken
if not for this Man I've never met.

I no longer stand before wrath,
for in my place is the blameless Man;
but He doesn't run or hunch over,
He steps into the fire with confidence.

He doesn't flinch at the sentence,
and instead walks over to where I sit;
He grips my hand as I cry out,
trembling with guilt and misery.

But with a face full of joy,
He explains how much He loves me;
this Man I do not know exclaims
how He will gladly die for me.

"Forgive me," I cry, unable to stop,
wishing I had chosen to live
a different life of purity instead of
this one that is death-worthy.

"Peace be with you," He says,

eyes gentle and voice calm;

a love fills His tone to the brim,

one capable of conquering my sin.

I watch as the Man is taken away;

in chains, He leaves, taking all

my vileness and disdain, bearing

the penalty I should've received.

Instead, I'm the one walking free;

and with every breath in my lungs,

every beat of my heart, I promise

to no longer choose impurity.

My death penalty was paid,

and nothing I could've done

would've been able to save me;

and now I live for the One.

The Man Who stole

my suffering.

That is His only crime,

a thief of death;

stealing away wrath,

all to give us righteousness.

He is the truest hero,

guilty only of loving me

and saving my soul

to bring Him glory.

Devotional

"For all have sinned and fall short of the glory of God." Romans 3:23

Key Takeaway: We understand the Gospel by seeing our sin

A follower of Christ can't honestly claim to follow Christ unless he or she has been utterly shattered by their own sin. We can't be who God made us to be without understanding the lengths He went to restore us to His design *(John 3:16)*. The Gospel message is meaningless if one doesn't acknowledge one's need for a Savior. To believe in a life-changing hope, we must first understand what we were saved from—*our sin*. Every one of us is guilty of it, and all deserve the penalty of death. But Jesus took our death sentence so we can live. The closer we come to Christ, the dirtier we tend to feel. Yet, in those moments of grief and repentance, we are being made clean. That's why knowing God is more important than "finding our true selves." We'll never be satisfied if our identity is found in anything other than Jesus. Knowing God more every day is how we'll learn to live and love like He does. Created by His hands, loved by His perfect heart, a life surrendered to God finds all it was made for. We are lost to our sins without Him, and that's what makes the Gospel so powerful. It's at His feet that we are freed and find our purpose and identity.

Open My Eyes

Lord, open my eyes,
help me see the light;
soften my heart and crack
this stone muscle of mine.

Renew my mind,
transform me from the inside;
God, I praise You,
I lift Your name high.

Jesus, You deserve all praise,
every eye, every tongue;
may all nations proclaim how
You are reigning over all things.

Oh God, I praise You,
may Your name be lifted high!
Soften my heart, Lord, open my eyes,
make me receptive to Your Word.

Use me to be a
guiding light.

Devotional

"But be doers of the word, and not hearers only, deceiving yourselves. For if anyone is a hearer of the word and not a doer, he is like a man who looks intently at his natural face in a mirror. For he looks at himself and goes away and at once forgets what he was like." James 1:22-24

Key Takeaway: Don't limit faith to privacy

If we've been transformed from the inside out, why aren't we telling everyone we can? This world cannot tolerate disagreements or truth. It's an offended society that exclaims inclusivity by excluding those it disagrees with. Living out faith isn't easy in a world set to destroy it.

We grow comfortable in our private prayers and moments with God, and we can ignore how desperate people are for the same. Finding time with God away from the world's distractions is crucial, but so is proclaiming the wonders of God to those who don't know Him. Fear has kept us quiet and docile for too long. If we want to live for God and love people like we claim to, how dare we keep this hope burning in our hearts to ourselves? It's our responsibility to proclaim the hope of the Gospel—an urgent message designed for those desperately seeking it. As followers of Christ, we are called not only to know God but to make Him known *(Acts 20:24)*.

Expectations

Expectations, so many stares,
voices vying for my attention;
I try to run away from them,
but I always end up nowhere.

People watch my every step.
One foul move and mistake,
they pinpoint them all;
they make sure I repent.

They calculate my faults,
ignore my strengths, while I
try to please them, but,
their answers remain the same.

"You're too weak."
"You won't survive this world."
"Why do you speak?"
"Your goals are so blurred."

"No one cares."
"Just stay silent and listen."

"Your accomplishments mean nothing."
"All you do is worthless."

Expectations.
How terrifying they can be
when the truth isn't far;
their words don't lie, not really.

I *am* weak, on my own;
I can't be enough.
I try to fill this void, but seem
to return more empty than not.

I *give* and *do*, hoping to
please someone into
seeing that I can achieve
more than failures and dreams.

Expectations corner me
and isolation is their friend,
joining hands to pound me
with misery; they hound me.

I have eyes, and yet,

suddenly, I can't see.
I savor the lies of the
enemy.

They taste bitter on my tongue,
but I can't stop myself;
I drink the lies like water
as if somehow I'll be brighter.

Expectations destroy my plans.
I run as far as I can, but my legs
can't take it anymore, and I
fear I can't stand.

People pass me as I scream;
to the sky, I shout with force,
but no one spares me a glance.
Tears pour, and yet, I'm a ghost.

A shell of a girl
with no grounding purpose,
for my life was their applause
and now their hands have grown quiet.

But I hear their cheers
as they laugh and point at me,
gleeful to see tears while I
place my hands over my ears.

Yet the sounds penetrate deep,
tearing into my soul and mind;
rooting up all my joy and
replacing my identity with a lie.

"You'll never amount to anything."
"All your days will waste away."
"No one will enjoy what you're doing."
"Go hide and fade away."

My stomach churns, and my heart breaks,
for these lies have become a
familiar and gruesome taste.
When did I get to know them so well?

Expectations cloud my mind,
levels I'll never reach,
things I can't achieve to please;
I fear I will die.

My life was for them,

but now they hate me;

I have failed to please them.

What am I supposed to be doing?

Darkness scatters my soul

and I curl up, telling myself

I'm fine,

but at the end of the day…

I know I'm not.

I'm not okay, though I fight to be;

I can't achieve these things

people wish of me. My soul is

stretched thin, and I'm withering.

What purpose do I have if

I can't even please man?

How can I please God when

I've failed in all things?

Expectations don't count

how many grueling hours

I've tried, climbed, bled;
they don't see my efforts.

I can't please them,
no, not even a little.
I try so hard, but I fear
I've come to the end.

I must admit, I am so tired,
I think I'll give in;
they don't want me anyway,
why pretend?

Why act as if I can be something?
Why believe a lie of purpose?
Why chase after an empty dream?
Why hope in something I'm losing?

Quickly, their praise disappeared.
Love and adoration, how I craved them;
to be seen and known intimately,
but they've left me crippling.

I never asked them to expect me

to be something out of my ability;

I didn't ask to please them.

God, help me.

The fear of man.

What a treacherous thing;

so silly and small, yet,

the downfall of all.

If I were to simply turn my head,

into Your light,

I'd hear the joyous laughter;

I'd feel the weight lifted high.

At Your feet, all You expect

is for my heart to be bare as I repent;

so here it is, God, take every inch,

take it all and show me how to live.

Everything I needed

everything I couldn't be

everything I sought and

everything missing.

Resting in the palms of the One
Who created me;
You reach down and touch my heart,
sending my pulse soaring.

Expectations don't matter
in my Father's eyes,
for He's already fulfilled each one,
leaving us only to accept eternal life.

He doesn't point or laugh,
He hears my cries;
God takes my hand and
guides me away from the lies.

I don't hold back this time and
I accept Him inside,
fully surrendered and dedicated to
His marvelous design.

I don't run anymore
because I know Someone;
He sees me, knows me, and
has always loved me.

He saw the way my soul withered
beneath the expectations of takers;
He revived me and gave me life,
He showed me opinions vanish in time.

People don't get to name me,
my choices are my own;
but it's His grace that saved me,
His Spirit that has led me home.

It's His light inside of me
that draws me ever so close;
because of Him, I can do it,
I can find my way home.

The battle is excruciating,
for the lies haven't gone;
but now they're faced with the truth,
and I've witnessed true love.

I prayed and begged someone
would tell me I matter,
and today I've found that
it's You I'm after.

Expectations don't seem as scary
standing next to my King;
they're simply another stepping stone
to discover my dependence on Him.

Devotional

"For am I now seeking the approval of man, or of God? Or am I trying to please man? If I were still trying to please man, I would not be a servant of Christ."
Galatians 1:10

Key Takeaway: We live to please God, not man

Basing our worth on the opinions of others leads only to destruction. When we start believing the lies of who we're "supposed" to be, our identity in Christ is sabotaged, and we lose sight of Whose we are. The fear of man destroys the notion that our worth comes from Christ, not us. Fearing man is rooted not only in insecurity, but also in pride, as we strive to be *more* in an effort to be praised. We try to be enough, forgetting that Christ was already enough to satiate the wrath our sins need to be justified. The fear of man deflates the awe we should have towards God. Even doing good things like serving in church, communities, or giving of our resources for a cause that glorifies God can be done with the wrong intentions *(Matthew 6:1)*. The only fear we should have in our hearts is a reverent, awe-inspiring fear of the Lord. When the opinions and expectations of others begin to take priority in our actions and thoughts, we must remember that God doesn't expect anything of us except to fall at His feet in surrender.

I Prayed

I was lost in this dark hole,

searching for hope;

anxiety filled my soul,

and fear held me on a rope.

I was scared of the future,

of the unknown, my thoughts;

I'd lie awake at night,

my stomach in knots.

My mind was once safe and strong,

now it was my greatest enemy;

I couldn't help but think of my sin,

couldn't stop the thoughts pouring in.

Hours

days

months passed…

The anxiety was on and off,

I thought I was okay.

It wouldn't last, right?

Please, just one more day.

I didn't know if what I felt was

me

the devil

or God.

How could I recognize His voice

when I could barely recognize

my own dark and evil thoughts?

How could I know?

Everything was so fogged,

empty, cold, lost;

fear gripping me tight,

chaining me up like a dog.

I was screaming inside,

I wanted to cry;

in the crowd, I smiled, but,

I lied.

I tried to convince myself I was okay,

especially in bed, when

nightmares had all hands and
all I had was my head.

Reading was an escape
from the traps of shame;
writing was too, but,
only for a bit of the day.

I really was trying,
stumbling around and fighting;
but I still didn't know,
couldn't understand, *what was wrong?*

Why am I thinking these things?
Why is my blood cold?
Why does my heart race?
Why can't I sleep anymore?

Then, I prayed.

I prayed
and prayed
and prayed
and *prayed.*

On my knees, sobbing,

gripping my head and crying;

kicking my feet and praying,

begging for it all to end.

I'd have one-sided conversations

with God at the end of the day;

I said what I had to say,

then I was back to laughing.

Joy bursts,

anxiety pricks again;

a seesaw that felt like it'd

never end.

A constant war on my mind and soul.

Was I losing? Am I fighting?

What are the rules? Because

I have no weapons.

When would it end?

I'd read my Bible, my mind would drift;

my relationship with God, a sinking ship,

while a storm threatened to swell and
utterly capsize what little was left.

I would fake a smile and
my soul would shift,
so I prayed even more,
gasping for breath.

I prayed before reading His Word
I prayed during the storms
I prayed before sleeping
I prayed after waking.

Anxiety kept beeping,
but I found my sword;
I refused to give up and
grasped for more.

Then suddenly, You were everywhere.
Social media, church, my home;
everywhere I turned…
I saw Jesus.

I couldn't help but stare.

Is this what it's like to
have a relationship with
the One Who cares?

My heart lurched.
I felt Him, *God;*
He took my heart again
and it began to revive.

He showed me what was wrong:
my sin.
A lukewarm pipe, I was
drowning in.

Diseased and stagnant like
a putrid stream of toxic waste;
bubbling and boiling until
everything around wasted away.

I could see the darkness in my life,
contrasted beside the Light;
yet, despite now knowing, I
still ignored Him and chose the night.

Anxiety grabbed my heart,
quick as a knife.
I cried for help, and to my surprise,
You never left my side.

He was there from the start,
the One making me strong.
You guarded my heart and
rewired my mind to fly.

I'd run
He'd follow
I'd plug my ears
He'd whisper a holler.

I would create an excuse,
but God knew I was
being used…
by sin, satan, and *me.*

I didn't realize I created an enemy
within my own body;
I didn't see the evil forces
I was constantly at war with.

God never gave up on me,
even when I didn't ask for help;
it was as if a shadow hung over me,
but God rescued this empty shell.

A husk I was,
empty and blowing with
a deceitful breeze;
tossed, crushed, crumbling.

There's more to believing in God,
more than asking for forgiveness;
it's a profound gift of peace,
a race to righteousness.

How did I last so long
without knowing You, God?
How did I live life when
all I did was waste time?

I pray I never forget
Who You are,
for it's in You I find
who You've called me to be.

Devotional

"Do not be anxious about anything, but in everything by prayer and supplication with thanksgiving let your requests be made known to God." Philippians 4:6

Key Takeaway: Going to God is the best thing we can do

Our hardships can tempt us to draw away from God when they should bring us closer. They remind us of our need for a Savior and cause us to depend on God. This is why, as followers of Christ, we rejoice in suffering *(1 Peter 4:13)*, because it's on the darkest nights that we discover Who God is and who He says we are. When we are stripped of all, that's when we see Jesus is everything, and prayer is but a doorway into what God has planned.

Prayer isn't our last resort, nor should it be the "only thing left" to do. When we see prayer as the last option, we downplay the power of going to the Almighty. Calling on God and falling at His feet is not the least we can do; it's the *greatest*. Because it's at the feet of our Savior that we find true strength, peace, and joy. Instead of approaching prayer as our last step, it should be our first *(1 Thessalonians. 5:17)*. Taking things to God should always be first. Prayer isn't powerless or something small. Rather, it's a humble display of our awe in the Lord. When we truly pray and pour our hearts out to God, we are welcomed into His good plans.

Faithful

You called me out of
darkness into light;
You freed me from my chains,
and the fear inside.

You rescued me from
my darkest nights,
and I know You will
never leave my side.

You are faithful, God
Faithful, You are.

A breeze that guides,
and a tide that draws close;
a breath of life and a
path that leads home.

You are faithful, God
Faithful, You are.

Devotional

"If we are faithless, He remains faithful—for He cannot deny Himself."
2 Timothy 2:13

Key Takeaway: God's faithfulness is eternal

One of our greatest hopes is in the faithfulness of Jesus. It's easy to lose sight of this promise of eternal grace when we battle things that often take precedence over promises. Yet, even then, God's faithfulness is made known. Just like the Israelites in the wilderness, and all the others who turned from worshipping God to worship idols, when we stumble and ignore Who God is, it doesn't change *Who He's always been (Hebrews 13:8).* He isn't struck by our behavior or unsure how to handle our mistakes or lack of capability. Instead, He uses everything that makes us fall short and transforms us into a tool to further His kingdom.

Our unfaithfulness doesn't affect the faithfulness of God, though Jesus says in *John 15:4, "Abide in me, and I in you."* A relationship with God has to go both ways. If we're not trying to remain faithful to God, then we are faithfully following someone or something else. But praise God, even when we follow evil, He never fails to lead us back home. Nothing can separate us from Him when He's called us by name.

Who You Are

What do I do?
I feel far from You
and I don't know why,
yet, I know what I've done.

Caught in this life,
in the haste of society.
"Do this, do that."
What is wrong with me?

After all this time,
you'd think I'd know to
place my precious life into
the hands of the Lord.

I try
so hard
to live a life dedicated to
Who You are.

You've brought me so far.

But I am
failing daily,
and all I can do is
trust You to save me.

What do I do now?
Why do I forget how
to live, when life has me
hanging upside down in sin?

Oh God, remind me
how to live for You,
when the world tries to
tear me away from You.

How dare I ask,
and grovel at Your feet,
for something I've asked for
over and over?

How dare I beg
for Your guidance
when I constantly let
the world take over?

How can I plead for
Your love when
all I do is…
push it aside?

Oh God, thank You
for Who You are;
free me from
this life.

This life of letting
fear run rampant,
and sin lay sleeping
beneath my skin.

This life where I
jump right into traps,
and keep letting the enemy
run free in my head.

Free me from this life;
show me how to take flight
on the wings of Your
mercy and grace.

Your power isn't
limited by me,
it's not waiting for
me to breathe.

Your power is what
gives me life;
it's what shows me
how to fly.

So I will trust in
Who You are,
and I will place my
whole heart in Your hands.

Regardless of how I cower,
You are greater than the
overwhelming and
soul-draining shame.

Freedom is Who You are
Life is Who You are
Joy is Who You are
Peace is Who You are.

Surrendered is who I am.

Devotional

"My flesh and my heart may fail, but God is the strength of my heart and my portion forever." Psalm 73:26

Key Takeaway: Who we are doesn't change Who God is

When our hearts aren't focused on God, we try to fill that "missing piece" with anything but Him. However, the moment we realize *Who God is*, nothing else compares. What the world has to offer is ashes next to the all-consuming fire of Who God is. We don't need a successful career, business, relationship, marriage, or lifestyle to be fulfilled. In fact, when we seek fulfillment in these things, we are filling a hole only God can overflow. These things aren't wrong, but like anything, they can take priority over our relationship with God. If we're not careful, we may start finding our identity in things the world has created, too. But what if we lost it all one day, like Job? Would God be enough? The truth is, God has always been enough *(Philippians 4:19)*. He fulfills every criterion our hearts long for. God is above all. If He weren't enough, Jesus' death wouldn't give us the freedom we have today. Instead, the question we need to ask is, "Do I put God first in all things to the point where, if I lost it all, He'd be enough for me?" When we are full in Christ, nothing can deprive us of Him.

Unashamed

God,
I don't want to be
ashamed of my testimony,
of that girl I was.

For her story is a
proclamation of
Your wonder-working
glory.

Make me unashamed.

I want to be unashamed
of the way You've changed
me from the inside out,
evident on the outer walls.

I want to be unashamed of
breaking apart at Your feet,
in tears and misery, because
it was then, I became whole.

I want to be unashamed of
those darkest nights when
my thoughts grew vile, and
my mind threatened to split.

I want to be unashamed of
the days when I felt
undeserving to live this life,
praying for the days to go by.

I want to be unashamed,
for the story of the girl I
used to be exudes Your love,
and the presence of Your mercy.

I am unashamed.

I am unashamed to tell
the whole world how
broken and lost I was;
how You saved my soul.

I am unashamed to confess
that I bore dirty thoughts,

days when I shriveled
and almost gave up.

I am unashamed to admit
that I questioned my faith,
and turned my back on
Your life-saving grace.

Because that's not where my
story ended, but where I found
You, Jesus;
when Your love saved me.

I am unashamed to tell
the whole world how You
opened my eyes to all the
sins in my life.

I am unashamed to confess
that I had a lukewarm faith
before I fell into grace, and
before You renewed my name.

I am unashamed to admit

that Jesus is my Lord and Savior,
King of the heavens and the earth;
the reason I'm here today.

I am unashamed to confess
that I need You, God,
every piece of me;
mind, heart, and soul.

I am unashamed.

Because You've taken
my shame on that cross,
defeated it for me so that
I can live today.

I am unashamed to tell
the whole world that I
love Jesus Christ, and that
my life's never been the same.

I am unashamed to confess
that I follow Him closely,
walking in His Spirit

until He calls me home.

I am unashamed to admit
that I look for Him everywhere,
searching for His touch and
the guiding sense in my soul.

God, help me be unashamed
of my testimony,
for it is infallible evidence of
Your mercy and glory.

Devotional

Key Takeaway: Our testimonies are evidence of God

There is a fear that attaches itself to a testimonial. The last thing our enemy wants is for us to give personal accounts of God's work in our lives. So we keep to ourselves. We ignore the nudge to open up and instead isolate ourselves, disregarding the honor of being able to share what God is doing in our lives. Or perhaps we don't think we have a testimony worth sharing. Leave it to those who have gone through *really* hard times. But every testimony has at least one thing in common: the redemption from sin *(Romans 3:23)*. If we don't share what God has saved us from, why did He save us from it? Jesus didn't transform our lives so we could cocoon away. He knew all He saved us from would ultimately glorify Him. Our testimony is evidence of the Gospel *(Romans 1:16)*. It proclaims that God does indeed save. Jesus changes lives, and this truth is told in the very seams of our stories. Every day is a testimony to God's grace, no matter how difficult or peaceful. Despite the fear and discomfort sharing a testimony can bring, proclaiming the works of God is always worth it.

Through His Eyes

How do I see myself
through the eyes of God
when all I see is my sinful self,
a fraud?

But more importantly,
how do I see others
through His eyes when
I despise looking at myself?

How do I show people grace,
like He did on the cross,
when I beat myself up
for every mistake I make?

How do I show forgiveness,
in a way that shows His goodness,
when I can't even rid
my own shame?

And how am I to love
"Thy neighbor as thyself"

if, when everything I see
in the mirror, I hate?

Oh God, help me see
myself through Your eyes;
to better love those around me,
to be a burning light.

You say, "Treat others the way you
want to be treated," but, Lord,
I fear I treat *myself* as the enemy
instead of satan.

I am frustrated with my sin,
aggravated by my weaknesses
and failures to live within
Your mighty hand.

Show me how to love myself
the way You did on the cross,
spilling Your blood, taking my sin,
even while I was still lost.

All I can see now is that sin,

though I know I'm no longer bound;
I'm no longer chained or restrained,
but rather, I've been forgiven.

I hate who I am when I
fall from the truth;
I hate how I can fail to
correctly represent You.

But God, You've redeemed me.
I'm no longer a sinner but a
sinner saved, evil no longer my name;
You've given me a new identity.

How do I escape the enemy's lies,
even though I know the truth?
How do I keep on fighting when I
forget sin has no hold on me?

I shall look above,
to my perfect Savior,
for it's in You alone
I find what I was made for.

I am set apart,
because You were
torn apart.

I am chosen,
because Your blood
coats my skin.

I am set free,
because You defeated
all my enemies.

I am loved,
because You created me
to be with You.

I am a light, for You shine
through me, and I am salt
for You transform my heart
and produce good fruits in me.

God, help me see myself
through Your eyes,
not my human faults

but all You've made me to be.

God, help me to see the good
that is You in me;
help me see how You
designed me to be.

Truly, all I have to love
about myself are things
not of my own doing, but
of Your saving.

Help me love the parts of me
that exude Your beauty and
relentless mercy; show me how I am,
in Your eyes, a masterpiece.

For all I have to love
about myself
is not me, but,
You in me.

So God, when I am tempted to
hate and despise myself,

remind me of Whose I am;

remind me of my identity.

Teach me how to see myself

through Your eyes, Jesus,

so in turn, I can better be, on this

earth, an example of Your goodness.

Guide me in love,

and show me how to

do the same.

Help me see me

through the eyes of

my Designer.

Who am I to hate

that which You created?

Who am I to judge

that which You saved?

And who am I to tear apart

the already broken pieces

of a life You died for to make

this stone heart receptive?

Who am I to shatter
the one You love, God?
Who am I to break the one
You've put back together?

Oh, how You love me,
the wretched sinner I am;
Oh, how You saved me,
a grace I can't understand.

Through His eyes,
all He sees is His Son,
battered and bruised for
all who have fallen.

Through His eyes,
He sees I am covered in
His blood, protected from wrath,
saved by His Son.

Through His eyes,
my sin is wiped clean,

not because of me but

because of mercy.

Through His eyes,

I am not perfect, but,

I have been perfectly saved

by Him.

Devotional

"For in Christ Jesus you are all sons of God, through faith." Galatians 3:26

Key Takeaway: When we hate ourselves, we attack God's creation

As followers of Christ, being hard on ourselves is a byproduct of imperfection. But instead of hating sin and the enemy, we end up hating ourselves. We forget grace is supposed to be applied not only to others, but to *us*, too *(Titus 2:11)*. Hating who God designed us to be—not what the world says to be—means we hate God's creation. When we insult ourselves, we're essentially insulting God, as if He made a mistake in creating us. But we cannot forget that, before the Fall, God's design for mankind was good *(Genesis 1:31)*. We're made in His image, all of us. Our identity can't be compared to anything else and is attacked every day by our sinful nature. Yet, thanks to Jesus, His perfection is enough to cover our imperfections. There is a time and place for repentance and forgiveness. Both are paramount to following Christ *(1 John 1:9)*. It's not true repentance if we come only for forgiveness, and it's not true forgiveness if we come only to repent and dwell on the past. We need to repent with our whole hearts and accept God's forgiveness to be changed.

Sunsets and Covenants

As I lingered on Your glory revealed,
between the thinning clouds against
the pinks and blues of sunset,
I was left standing in awe.

My mind traveled back many years ago,
when You were arrested for the
crimes and sins of a transgressor;
swapped for a criminal to be freed.

I thought of Barabbas,
wondered about his heart and mind.
What did he think when he saw
my Savior take those 39?

Did he weep, knowing
an innocent Man was condemned
because of his own undoing?
Did he stand with the crowd, jeering?

Did Barabbas attempt to free that
blameless Man on Calvary? Or

did he demand Him to be stoned and
imprisoned with the rest of them?

Yet, Barabbas is far from a
man sentenced to history,
for is he not all of us today?
Those of us who follow blasphemy.

What do we do?

When our Savior is mocked
and blasphemed in our
very neighborhoods and
our own communities?

Do we take a stand and
fight for the purity of Jesus'
name and holy identity?
Or do we hide in the crowd?

Do we cower,
no better than the enemy?

What do we do when

His perfect truth is twisted and
contorted into evil phrases that
please man and make him famous?

Do we look through the
lens of God's Word or
do we welcome the world
with open arms?

I am Barabbas.

A criminal.
A thief.
A liar.
A cheat.

But in my place,
on that cross,
where *I* should be,
is *Jesus.*

In *my* place
bearing *my* shame
taking *my* guilt and blame...

Is my *King*.

Above, I gaze upon Him,

bleeding and wounded;

dying from the pressure of

being nailed to a cross.

I'm being pushed further

from seeing this sacrifice

as I drown in the crowd,

deeper and deeper until I'm lost.

I let them shove me back;

I let them keep me from You,

because I fear I don't deserve

to witness Your truth.

I fear people knowing

that I'm the reason You're there;

I fear proclaiming my love

despite how much You suffered.

Tears flood my eyes as

they mock Your name,

torturing You still
while I hide in fear.

Give me the strength
to step out of the crowd,
to boldly proclaim my faith,
to refuse to back down.

I am Barabbas.

And in my place
is the One Who
has saved me with
undeserved grace.

Devotional

"If the world hates you, know that it has hated Me before it hated you." John 15:18

Key Takeaway: We need to be bold and firm in our faith

When God's name is profaned, we can often slip into the crowd, too afraid to take a stand. We become complacent, agreeable, and tolerant. Because, if we're honest, we don't want to be hated. We want to be loved by the world, friends, and family. But the more we hide in the crowd and applaud with the other scorners, the harder our hearts become. When we aren't actively taking a stand against the lies, the truth blurs, until we don't even know what we believe anymore. We begin to neglect God's Word and become consumed by the world.

To portray Jesus' character, we need to abide in it. And we can only be who He's called us to be when we leave behind who we once were *(Matthew 16:24)*. Just like those who jeer for Jesus to be crucified, we are no better if we refuse to stand firm in our faith. The world is promised to hate us, but defeat comes when we begin to hate like the world and toss aside the love of Christ for a feeble replacement. The life God gives is everlasting and shouldn't make us cower in fear, but rather, it should push us to lean on God, boldly in courage.

Darkest Hour

Alone, You were,
whipped and beaten
in the dark;
broken and mistreated.

In Your darkest hour,
Lord, they left You
alone, while You were
to be tortured.

You knew this, though,
that Your closest friends
would leave You and
disown You.

You knew Peter would
deny You three times,
and still, You chose him.

You knew Judas would
betray You for coin,
and still, You loved him.

You knew in Your
darkest hour
all Your dear friends
would betray You.

And still,
You chose them.

Forgive me, Jesus,
for leaving You when
I should be running
towards You.

Forgive me, Lord,
for denying You
when shame should
be unwelcome here.

Forgive me, God,
for departing from
Your side, like the disciples
did on Your darkest night.

In the face of death,

as You prepared for
torture, the drinking of
the cup fixed for You.

Alone, You stood at
the door of wrath,
for my sins and all
the ones to come after.

In Your darkest hour,
You were the greatest
light and sacrifice;
the greatest power.

Abandoned, You were;
left behind, while we
turned our backs and
chose the plight.

Still, You pursued,
after all this time;
You knew me and
Your love survived.

When I run away,
when I am faithless;
when I give You up
for nothing but coin,

You remain.

You pursue me and
turn me back, like
Gomer and Israel,
those often misled.

You rekindled
a flame once dead,
for You are life,
the reason we live.

In Your darkest hour
You remained faithful,
knowing how You'd be
hated and deserted.

In my darkest hour
You remained faithful,

even when my eyes turned,

even when I was depleted.

For it's on these

darkest hours of life that

I've learned it's in You

true joy takes flight.

Devotional

"For the LORD loves justice; He will not forsake His saints. They are preserved forever, but the children of the wicked shall be cut off." Psalm 37:28

Key Takeaway: God doesn't abandon us

No matter how often we turn from God, if He has chosen us, we can't outrun His love. Like the prodigal son, He welcomes us with open arms when we repent of how we've fallen. Even amid desertion and abandonment, God's love and faithfulness have always persisted. In His darkest hour, facing what we deserved, Jesus still cried out to God, *"Father, forgive them, for they know not what they do." Luke 23:34*. He prayed for His enemies while *He* was the one suffering. On the cross, dying and bleeding, His heart was set towards God and mercy because of His love *for us*.

We can try to run from Him, but God chose us for *His glory (Ephesians 1:12).* Though we can participate in prayer and be a part of God's will, there is nothing we can do to change it, just like there's nothing we can do to save ourselves. This is a great comfort to us, for when we grasp that our sins are wiped clean by Someone Who bore no guilt for them, our perspectives shift. Jesus knows what it's like to be betrayed, but what's even greater is that He also knows how to perfectly love us, even on the darkest days.

Who I Was

It's as though the world
had slowly shifted into
something more beautiful
right before my eyes.

I didn't notice
until I was living it,
this beautiful life
no longer filled with lies.

A year has gone
since I was suffocated
by crippling fear and
anxiety.

It's been a year
since last I let the
devil have a hold
on my very identity.

If you told that girl,
from three years ago,

she'd be free to
live and breathe

I think she would've
laughed and told you
that's silly, for anxiety
is what I am. It's *me.*

But now I sit here
and pour my heart out
with a calm pulse,
overjoyed that I'm free.

Anxiety doesn't define me,
no, not even fear;
a year has passed since then
and I'm still here.

Though I've come close
to freezing until numb,
I never gave in, no,
God has made me strong.

Anxiety is not

my identity,

though it defined me

for too long.

Now my face and faith

rest in His purity;

the light of my Father,

an everlasting love.

A year long gone,

goodbye, who I was;

I won't miss how you broke,

only the time you stole.

Devotional

"Therefore, if anyone is in Christ, he is a new creation. The old has passed away; behold, the new has come." 2 Corinthians 5:17

Key Takeaway: We are made new in Christ

We can determine if we are following Christ and walking in the Spirit by how we're changed *(Romans 12:2)*. The whole point of God sending His Son to die for us is so that we'd no longer have to live as we used to. With Jesus, it's a new world, a new life, and a new purpose. If we remain living in sin, what, then, would His death on the cross be for? New life takes discipline, surrender, obedience, and a willingness to turn away from the things leading us astray.

Being made new in Christ is an inner change, a shift in our souls as the veil is removed from our eyes. And from this inner heart change, the things outside us follow suit. When we acknowledge and believe Jesus is Lord over our lives—when we dedicate our lives to living for Him—then we no longer partake in the things of this world. In fact, worldly things become less appealing over time. With these steps of obedience, we will find that the lives we once lived are completely transformed. It isn't instant but often a gradual shift. A progressive refinement that we walk through until eternity. The "made new" adventure.

Because of *Him*, who we are is no longer who we were.

Final Thoughts

Despite this book's short length, I pray you grew even the tiniest bit. I know I did while writing this. The more the words flowed, the more I was reminded that my identity isn't about me at all, but *Him (Philippians 1:21)*. *Who I Was* only captures the surface of God's relentless love and pursuit of us. To better understand that love and our identity in Christ, we need to continually abide in Him and draw closer to Him. The more we learn and listen to His voice, the better we can differentiate what He says rather than listening to what the world screams *(John 10:27)*.

Life is more than us.

It's Him. He is life.

To truly discern who we're meant to be, we need to look at the cross and witness Who God has always been. We are nothing without Him, just floating shells attempting to be filled by decaying substitutes. But with Him, we are more than conquerors, warriors destined to triumph in the face of adversity. As followers of Christ, we must be careful not to elevate ourselves into a posture of arrogance, any more than we must utterly destroy who God calls us to be in Jesus. If you struggle to love yourself like Jesus loves you, or fail to give yourself grace and forgiveness, you are not alone. If there's one thing I pray you take away from this book, it's this: the answer to any question—self-worth, identity, freedom, peace—is found in Christ *(John 14:6)*. We may not know everything, but the things we're meant to, the things God wants us to know, can only be found at His feet. Our relationship with Christ enables us to have better relationships with others and with ourselves.

If you refuse to believe you are loved even after reading *Who I Was*, then, my dear friend, I encourage you to return to the cross—something we did often in this book. Do not forfeit Jesus' sacrifice, which portrayed a love so great that not even death could contain it. Do not take for granted an offering so pure that sin couldn't taint it.

We *are* loved.

Not because of who we are but because of Who God is.

And that, my dear friend, is even sweeter.

"'For the mountains may depart and the hills be removed, but my steadfast love shall not depart from you, and my covenant of peace shall not be removed,' says the LORD, who has compassion on you."
Isaiah 54:10

Notes of Gratitude

Thank You, God, for the wisdom and guidance You continuously pour into me. Thank You for giving me an everlasting identity through the death and resurrection of Jesus Christ. Thank You for being all I need. I love You.

Mom and Dad, I thank God for building me up in a home where I could be supported and feel safe to be my nerdy, weird self. And to mum specifically (to stay with the "woman" theme), I hope you know God used you as an example of a strong woman so that I could learn to be the same in Him. I love you both.

My sisters (in-laws included), we've had many opportunities to exercise our worth and identities in Christ. We've laughed, cried, glared in the mirror, grimaced at photos of ourselves, but always ended the day with God standing beside us. I pray this book reminds you of who you are in Christ. I love you all.

My nieces, watching you grow into your personalities reminds me why loving ourselves is so important. Not to elevate our egos or arrogance but to share in gratitude for the ways God reveals Himself through our laughter, smiles, giggles, and gentle touch. I pray this book settles deep in your hearts as you grow into women. Never forget that God is and always will be where your identity can be found. I love you, goofballs.

My friends, you were some of my greatest inspirations for this book. Hearing you reflect on insecurities and the hurtful things you would say about yourselves nudged me to dive into what it means to find our identities in Christ. I thank God for your friendships and pray we all come to fully believe how loved and cherished we are in the eyes of our Father. You are beautiful, loved, and redeemed, because He is wonderful. I love each of you, always.

To my dear friend, Addi, I felt compelled to give you your own acknowledgment for all the powerful conversations God has stirred between us. He has used your friendship in ways I never knew a friendship could be used. Thank you for pointing me back to Christ and walking alongside me as we grow in faith. Thank you for speaking truth when I was tempted to believe the lies. And thank you for planting the idea of combining devotionals and poetry (look how lovely it turned out!). I couldn't have asked a more fitting person to write the foreword to this book. I love you.

To my beta readers and those who read *Who I Was* while it

was still in a PDF, the time you sacrificed to study and immerse yourselves in this book truly warms my heart. Thank you for your suggestions and keen eyes. Without you, this book wouldn't be as polished as it is today!

And to my dear readers, I pray this book reminds you that your worth comes from Christ alone, and that is enough. No matter what people say or how you're perceived, no matter how much you hate yourself, if you've given your life to God, you are, without a doubt, loved. Thank you for reading *Who I Was*, my dear friend. May we step into the next day with hope, trusting God will transform us into who He designed us to be. We are His, and He is good. Let's live and love like it.

About the Author

Julia Rose is a multi-genre author passionate about glorifying God in story form. She published her first book at 21 in August of 2024—*He Is Faithful In Every Season*. With God's guidance, Julia aims to transform the world of literary entertainment one chapter at a time, whether it be poetry, nonfiction, fantasy, or contemporary romance. When Julia isn't writing, she's often daydreaming in the Florida heat, reading too many books, or spending time with loved ones.

Find more information about the author on her website at www.juliarosebooks.com

Support Julia's Ministry and <u>Leave A Review</u> Wherever Books Are Sold!

Amazon, Goodreads, Barnes & Noble, and other worldwide retailers

www.ingramcontent.com/pod-product-compliance
Lightning Source LLC
Chambersburg PA
CBHW051320120626
46547CB00015B/2316